Avala

Alan Gibbons

Illustrated by
Trevor Parkin

OXFORD
UNIVERSITY PRESS

Dad looked worried. "I think we're lost." We were half way up the mountain. It was snowing hard and we had lost the other climbers.

Something hit the ground. It was a rock.

Then more pieces of rock landed beside it in the snow. At that moment, there was an angry sound. It was like thunder. There was snow too. Bursts of white, powdery snow were falling around us.

Dad stopped.

"Avalanche!" he cried. "Run! Look out!"

We raced across the rocky ground. The rocks just kept coming. Sometimes we had to turn and twist as we ran.

It was like a deadly game of dodge ball. Terror filled me. The whole world seemed to be falling in on us.

"Look out!" Dad cried. A huge wall of snow, rocks and earth was coming. "Run! Just don't stop."

He tried to push me out of the way of the biggest rocks. That was the last thing Dad did before the snow hit him. Then he was gone. A moment later the snow hit me too.

Over and over I fell, like a rag doll. Snow was in my mouth. It was in my ears. It was pressing down on me.

Boom, went the snow, boom, boom inside my head. Still I fell. Pieces of snow, rock and earth punched me like fists.

I was being thrown about by thousands of tons of snow.

"You're going to die," I thought.

Then I blacked out.

When I came round I was in a small, dark space. The rocks had piled up on one side of me. They made a kind of cave in the snow. Suddenly everything went quiet.

I hurt all over but more than that, I felt pure fear.

"Dad," I said, very low and scared. There was no sound. "Dad, can you hear me?"

There was still no sound. Where was he? Was he OK? I did my best to move but it was hard. It was as if the world was on top of me.

I tried to remember what Dad told me. There was only one word in my head.
Dig.

So I pulled out some rocks and dug as hard as I could. It was so difficult, too difficult maybe, but still I kept going.

In the light of my torch, the world was white. The world was snow.

I just dug. I pushed my fingers through the snow and dug. My gloves were all ripped and my fingers were blue. There was no feeling in them.

Then I saw something.

It was a glove sticking through the rubble and snow. It had to be Dad. I had to get to him. I couldn't give up. I couldn't let him die.

I don't know how long I dug through the snow.

I found his arm then his leg, but it was trapped under a rock. At last I saw his face.

"Dad," I said. "Are you all right?"

I shook him and he blinked.

"I can't move," he said. He was pale and his lips were blue. The rock on his legs was big. Too big for me to move.

"Maybe I should go for help," I said.

"I don't know," he said. "You might get lost. Is your tracker working?"

"Yes," I said. "The bleeper's on."

"Then we've got a chance."

So I lay next to him. I tried to keep him warm.

"Hang on," I said. "Just hang on."

Then I heard a sound. Boom. It was over my head.

"It's the avalanche!" I said.

"No! Listen! I can hear something," Dad said. I could hear voices and then the sound of digging. Boom.

I know they were digging slowly but even a small sound seemed loud.

"Please," I begged, "don't make another avalanche." But they didn't. The sound became sharp, like a spade or a pick. Then a metal blade cut through the snow. It took a long time to dig us out.

For the first time, since the avalanche,
I saw the sun, then a face.

We were free.